# THE CANADIAN BRASS
# CHRISTMAS CAROLS
## 15 EASY ARRANGEMENTS
### ARRANGED BY LLOYD LARSON

**Using the Arrangements**
A music director/conductor can come up with various approaches to a carol. For instance: verse 1–no brass; verse 2–brass (Standard Version); verse 3–brass (Variation Verse); verse 4–brass (Standard Version) with Trumpet Descant. Or, another example might be: verse 1–brass (Standard Version) with keyboard; verse 2–brass (Standard Version); no keyboard; verse 3–brass (Variation Verse). Get creative!

**Optional Trumpet Descant**
An optional trumpet descant may be added to any of the Standard Version verses of a carol, available in the following Hal Leonard publication:  50484041 *The Canadian Brass Book of Christmas Trumpet Descants*

**Visit the official website of The Canadian Brass:**
**www.canbrass.com**

HAL•LEONARD®
CORPORATION
7777 W. BLUEMOUND RD. P.O. BOX 13819 MILWAUKEE, WI 53213

Visit Hal Leonard Online at
**www.halleonard.com**

# ANGELS WE HAVE HEARD ON HIGH

Traditional French carol, 18th C.

Traditional French melody, 18th C.

**STANDARD VERSION**
**Regally (♩ = 88)**

Repeat as needed (opt.)

**VARIATION VERSE**

(rit.)*

* *rit.* is used only if the Variation Verse is played as the final verse

*Return to Standard Version as needed*

50484037
The Canadian Brass Christmas Carols - 2

# AWAY IN A MANGER

Unknown author vs. 1 and 2
John Thomas McFarland vs. 3

James R. Murray, 1887

* *rit.* is used only if the Variation Verse is played as the final verse

*Return to Standard Version as needed*

# THE FIRST NOEL

Traditional English carol

Traditional English carol

**STANDARD VERSION**

Tenderly (♩ = 88)

_mf_

5

11

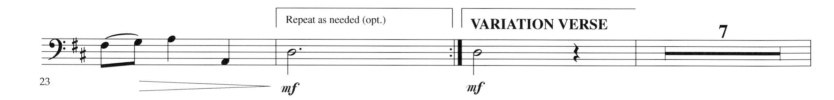

17

_f_

Repeat as needed (opt.)    **VARIATION VERSE**    7

23    _mf_    _mf_

32    _mp_ < _mf_

3

37    _mf_ < _f_

44    _ff_    (_rit._)*

* _rit._ is used only if the Variation Verse is played as the final verse

_Return to Standard Version as needed_

50484037
The Canadian Brass Christmas Carols - 4

# GO TELL IT ON THE MOUNTAIN

Words by John W. Work, Jr.

African-American Spiritual

* *rit.* is used only if the Variation Verse is played as the final verse

Return to Standard Version as needed

# GOOD CHRISTIAN FRIENDS, REJOICE

**Medieval Latin carol**

IN DULCI JUBILO
**Traditional German melody, 14th C.**

**STANDARD VERSION**
**Joyously (♩. = ca. 84)**

*mf*

5

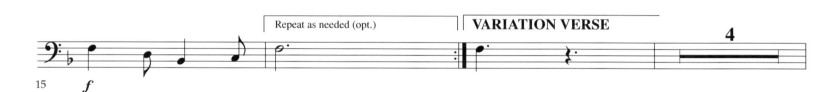

10

*cresc.*

Repeat as needed (opt.) | **VARIATION VERSE**

4

15 *f*

21 *mf*

25

29

*(cresc. e rit.)** *f*

* *rit.* is used only if the Variation Verse is played as the final verse

*Return to Standard Version as needed*

# HARK! THE HERALD ANGELS SING

Charles Wesley

Felix Mendelssohn

**STANDARD VERSION**
**Joyously** (♩ = ca. 100)

**VARIATION VERSE**

\* *rit.* is used only if the Variation Verse is played as the final verse

*Return to Standard Version as needed*

# IT CAME UPON THE MIDNIGHT CLEAR

**Edmund H. Sears**

**Richard Storrs Willis**

**STANDARD VERSION**
Flowing   (♩. = ca. 52)

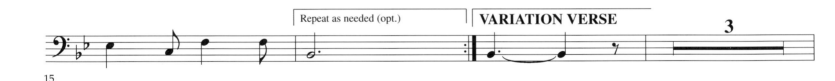

\* *rit.* is used only if the Variation Verse is played as the final verse

*Return to Standard Version as needed*

50484037
The Canadian Brass Christmas Carols - 8

# JOY TO THE WORLD

Isaac Watts

ANTIOCH
George F. Handel

**STANDARD VERSION**
**Joyously** ($\flat$ = ca. 88)

Repeat as needed (opt.)

**VARIATION VERSE**

* *rit.* is used only if the Variation Verse is played as the final verse

*Return to Standard Version as needed*

50484037
The Canadian Brass Christmas Carols - 9

# O COME, ALL YE FAITHFUL

Latin hymn,
attributed to John F. Wade

ADESTE FIDELES
John F. Wade's Cantus Diversi, 1751

* *rit.* is used only if the Variation Verse is played as the final verse

*Return to Standard Version as needed*

# O COME, O COME, EMMANUEL

Latin hymn, 12th C.

VENI EMMANUEL
based on Plainsong

* *rit.* is used only if the Variation Verse is played as the final verse

*Return to Standard Version as needed*

50484037
The Canadian Brass Christmas Carols - 11

# O LITTLE TOWN OF BETHLEHEM

**Phillips Brooks**

ST. LOUIS
Lewis H. Redner

\* *rit.* is used only if the Variation Verse is played as the final verse

*Return to Standard Version as needed*

50484037
The Canadian Brass Christmas Carols - 12

# ONCE IN ROYAL DAVID'S CITY

Cecil F. Alexander

**IRBY**
Henry J. Gauntlett

**STANDARD VERSION**
Regally  (♩ = ca. 96)

**VARIATION VERSE**

* *rit.* is used only if the Variation Verse is played as the final verse

*Return to Standard Version as needed*

# SILENT NIGHT

Joseph Mohr

STILLE NACHT
**Franz Gruber**

**STANDARD VERSION**
Gently ($\bullet$= ca. 36-40)

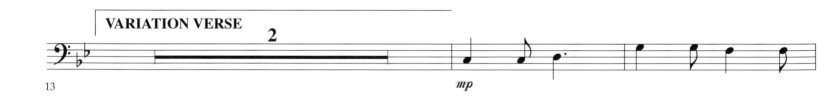

**VARIATION VERSE**

\* *rit.* is used only if the Variation Verse is played as the final verse

*Return to Standard Version as needed*

50484037
The Canadian Brass Christmas Carols - 14

# WE THREE KINGS

John H. Hopkins, Jr.

KINGS OF ORIENT
John H. Hopkins, Jr.

* *rit.* is used only if the Variation Verse is played as the final verse

*Return to Standard Version as needed*

# WHAT CHILD IS THIS?

William C. Dix

GREENSLEEVES
Traditional English melody, 16th C.

**STANDARD VERSION**
With gentle motion ( ♩. = ca. 46 )

* *rit.* is used only if the Variation Verse is played as the final verse

*Return to Standard Version as needed*